A FAMILY GUIDE TO

PRINCE CASPIAN

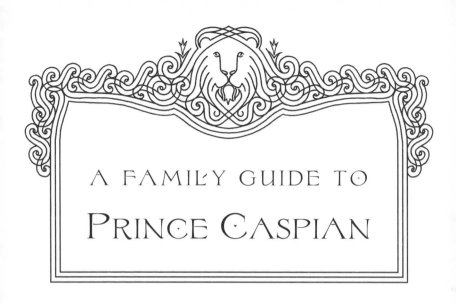

A FAMILY GUIDE TO
PRINCE CASPIAN

CHRISTIN DITCHFIELD

CROSSWAY BOOKS
WHEATON, ILLINOIS

A Family Guide to Prince Caspian
Copyright © 2008 by Christin Ditchfield

Published by Crossway Books
    a publishing ministry of Good News Publishers
    1300 Crescent Street
    Wheaton, Illinois 60187

Illustrations: Justin Gerard, Portland Studios, Inc.
Typesetting by Lakeside Design Plus
First printing, 2008
Printed in the United States of America

Library of Congress Cataloging-in-Publication Data
Ditchfield, Christin.
        A family guide to Prince Caspian / Christin Ditchfield.
                p. cm.
        Includes bibliographical references.
        ISBN 978-1-58134-844-6 (tpb)
        1. Lewis, C. S. (Clive Staples), 1898–1963. Prince Caspian. 2. Children's stories,
English—History and criticism. 3. Christian fiction, English—History and criticism. 4. Fantasy fiction, English—History and criticism. 5. Narnia (Imaginary place)
6. Christianity in literature. I. Title.

PR6023.E926P763 2008
823.009'9282—dc22

                                                                                    2007024072

CH   18   17   16   15   14   13   12   11   10   09   08
12   11   10   9   8   7   6   5   4   3   2   1

CONTENTS

I was seven years old when I was introduced to the Chronicles of Narnia. My aunt gave me a copy of the first book, *The Lion, the Witch and the Wardrobe*, for Christmas one year. Little did I know that it would have a profound and lasting impact on my life. I quickly devoured the entire Narnia series: *The Magician's Nephew*, *Prince Caspian*, *The Horse and His Boy*, *The Voyage of the Dawn Treader*, *The Silver Chair*, and *The Last Battle*. Though they were first published more than fifty years ago, the books are perennial best sellers, widely regarded as "classic literature," and consistently ranked among the greatest children's books ever written.

As a child, I read each of the books more than a dozen times, until they literally fell apart. Every time I read them, I enjoyed them more. And I discovered, as millions of others have, that there is far more to the Chronicles of Narnia than meets the eye. There are stories within the stories. The Chronicles of Narnia are full of hidden truths, deep mysteries, and spiritual treasures.

C. S. Lewis insisted that the Chronicles are not allegories, though many people have described them as such. Technically speaking, this is true. In an allegory, every character and event is a symbol of something else. Many of the characters and events in Narnia do not represent anything in particular—they are simply elements of the wonderful and fantastic adventures Lewis created. But many characters and events *do* represent something else, something from the spiritual realm. And although Lewis did not initially intend to write stories that would illustrate the most vital truths of the Christian faith, that is essentially what he did.

Jesus said, "Out of the abundance of the heart the mouth speaks" (Matthew 12:34, ESV). Consciously, and perhaps at times even unconsciously, Lewis wound powerful biblical truths through every chapter, every scene in the Chronicles of Narnia. It's not just the salvation story retold in *The Lion, the Witch and the Wardrobe*. Each of Lewis's books has deeply spiritual and profoundly scriptural content. His faith naturally found its expression in everything he wrote.

In *The Voyage of the Dawn Treader* (book 5), the Great Lion Aslan tells the two Pevensie children that their adventures in Narnia have come to an end; they will not be returning to this country again. Edmund and Lucy are horribly upset:

"It isn't Narnia, you know," sobbed Lucy. "It's you. We shan't meet you there. And how can we live, never meeting you?"

"But you shall meet me, dear one," said Aslan.

"Are—are you there too, Sir?" said Edmund.

"I am," said Aslan. "But there I have another name. You must learn to know me by that name. This was the very reason why you were brought to Narnia, that by knowing me here for a little, you may know me better there."

Years ago, after reading this passage in *Dawn Treader*, a little girl named Hila wrote to C. S. Lewis asking him to tell her Aslan's "other" name. Lewis responded, "Well, I want you to guess. Has there ever been anyone in this world who (1) arrived at the same time as Father Christmas, (2) Said he was the son of the Great Emperor, (3) Gave himself up for someone else's fault to be jeered at and killed by wicked people, (4) came to life again, (5) Is sometimes spoken of as a lamb (see the end of *Dawn Treader*). Don't you really know His name in this world? Think it over and let me know your answer."

Just as Edmund and Lucy's adventures in Narnia helped them come to know Aslan (Jesus) better, our adventures in Narnia can do the same for us. But sometimes, like little Hila, we may miss the deeper truths behind the stories.

This book is written to help readers identify and understand some of the many spiritual treasures in *Prince Caspian*. If you're new to Narnia, start with "About C. S. Lewis"—meet the beloved creator of the fantastic, fairy-tale world. As you read about the life and times of this extraordinary man, you'll find that many of the details of his stories take on a new and special significance. Then in "Inspiration, Imagination, and Adventure," learn more about where Lewis found his inspiration, where he got some of the ideas that inspired the Chronicles of Narnia and the story of *Prince Caspian*.

In "The Story within the Story," we'll take a closer look at the spiritual truths and scriptural symbolism in Lewis's story. This section is meant to be read side by side with the original book. For every chapter, you will find a key verse that reflects one of the primary spiritual themes. You'll also find a list of biblical parallels and principles. In some cases this list shows which events in Narnia are similar or even identical to stories in the Bible. In other cases it indicates where a particular element of Lewis's story illustrates an important scriptural principle. Each chapter concludes with an interesting fact or point to ponder and some additional Scriptures you can read, related to a previously-mentioned topic. Interspersed in these chapters, you'll find a series of "bonus chapters"—reflections or meditations that develop and expand on important biblical truths.

Parents, grandparents, and teachers who are reading along with their children may want to use this material to help start thoughtful discussion or extend story time into Scripture reading and family devotions. It's probably best not to attempt to cover all of the material offered in each and every chapter. Instead, choose one or two points that seem most interesting and meaningful to you, and go from there. (The bonus chapters work well as read-aloud devotionals.)

In "Continuing the Adventure," you'll discover many different ways to cook and eat apples, just as the Pevensies did when they were stranded on the island. Make your own mosaic or mural, like the ones in Aslan's How. Find ways to express your thoughts and feelings about the story. And learn more about the wonderful adventures that await you in the other books in the Chronicles of Narnia.

It is my hope and prayer that this book will help those who want to gain a deeper understanding and appreciation of *Prince Caspian* and the Chronicles of Narnia, and that having read this book, you will love the original all the more. Ultimately, may you find yourself developing an even deeper love for the source of Lewis's inspiration: The Word of God.

—Christin Ditchfield

ABOUT
C. S. LEWIS

Clive Staples Lewis was born on November 29, 1898, in Belfast, Northern Ireland. He never did like his name. When he was barely four years old, the precocious little boy changed his name to "Jacksie"; he absolutely refused to answer to anything else! Jack's older brother Warren—whom he nicknamed Warnie—was his constant companion and closest friend. The two boys spent countless hours exploring the gardens and forests and fields around their country home. On rainy days they climbed up into an old wardrobe and told each other stories about talking animals, magic kingdoms, knights, and dragons that lived in faraway lands.

Jack was only nine when his mother, Flora, was diagnosed with cancer. He fervently prayed for a miracle, pleading with God to heal her. But Flora did not get better. In fact, not long afterward she died. Jack felt abandoned and betrayed.

He turned his back on God completely, dismissing religion and the teachings of the church as foolishness.

A brilliant student, with a special gift for language and literature, Jack was awarded a scholarship to the prestigious University College at Oxford. He was not long in the classroom, however, before duty called him to enlist in the armed forces. World War I had begun, and Jack was sent to the front lines in France. Wounded in battle, he returned home less than a year later to complete his education. He became a college professor, teaching medieval and renaissance literature at Oxford. Lewis published several volumes of poetry and developed a reputation as a distinguished scholar and literary critic. About this time, he began engaging in heated intellectual debates with professors who were Christians, including fellow author J. R. R. Tolkien. These friends and coworkers challenged Lewis to rethink his beliefs. At the age of thirty-one, after a lengthy struggle, the avowed atheist became a devout Christian.

Much later Lewis wrote *Surprised by Joy*—a kind of spiritual autobiography that described his journey to faith. Then books such as *Mere Christianity*, *The Problem of Pain*, and *The Screwtape Letters* brought Lewis worldwide fame. In the 1950s, Lewis wrote a series of seven books for children, beginning with *The Lion, the Witch and the Wardrobe* and including *Prince Caspian*, which he called the Chronicles of Narnia. Immediately bestsellers, Lewis's fairy tales are now widely regarded as "classic literature" and considered to be among the greatest children's books ever written.

Lewis never had any children of his own. He remained a bachelor until the age of fifty-eight, when he met and married American writer Joy Davidman. When Joy died of cancer only four years later, Lewis looked after her two teenaged sons, Douglas and David. Though he felt the same hurt and anger and bitterness he had experienced after the loss of his mother, this time Lewis did not turn away from God. Instead, he turned to Him and found the strength to carry on. Lewis kept busy writing and speaking and—with the help of his brother Warnie—answering each one of the thousands of letters he received from fans around the globe.

On November 22, 1963, the world was reeling over the assassination of President John F. Kennedy. That same day, after a long illness, C. S. Lewis quietly passed away. But his life has continued to have an extraordinary impact on the world he left behind.

To date, C. S. Lewis's books have sold well over two hundred million copies and been translated into more than forty languages. He is routinely quoted by preachers and professors, presidents and prime ministers. Many of the most prominent leaders of the Christian faith today readily acknowledge having been profoundly influenced by the man *Time* magazine called "a young atheist poet who became one of the 20th century's most imaginative theologians."

Inspiration, Imagination, and Adventure

For C. S. Lewis, it all began with pictures in his head—startling visual images that gripped him, inspired him, and captured his imagination. Once—out of nowhere—he suddenly saw in his mind's eye a picture of a faun carrying an umbrella and parcels in a snowy wood. Lewis was only sixteen at the time. But more than thirty years later, he still remembered the scene he had so vividly imagined. By this time Lewis had become a world-famous author and lecturer. He decided he would try to write a story about the picture. He jotted down a few ideas in his notebook. As he thought about it, other pictures began to appear before him: a queen on a sledge and a magnificent lion.

"Suddenly Aslan came bounding in," Lewis later explained. "I don't know where the Lion came from or why

He came. But once He was there, He pulled the whole story together."

As he sat down to write the book that would become *The Lion, the Witch and the Wardrobe*—the first book in the Chronicles of Narnia—Lewis drew from many of his own real-life experiences. He recalled how he and his brother Warnie used to climb up into an old wardrobe and tell each other stories about talking animals, magic kingdoms, knights, and dragons. Much later, a little girl visiting Lewis's home asked him if there was anything *behind* the wardrobe he still kept there. Perhaps there was, Lewis thought. What if other worlds really did exist and you could get to them by stepping into a wardrobe? Lewis let his imagination soar.

A number of children had recently come to stay with Jack and Warnie and their housekeeper, Mrs. Moore. It was during World War II, and German fighter planes were conducting air raids against Great Britain. They dropped thousands of bombs on the most heavily populated cities. Whenever possible, parents sent their children to live with friends and relatives out in the country, where it was safer.

Of course, Lewis had no children of his own, and he hadn't really spent any time with young people in years. But as he got to know the children who stayed in his home, Lewis discovered something that alarmed him. These children didn't seem to know how to entertain themselves. They didn't have much imagination at all. They didn't read. And they were in way too much of a hurry to become adults. These children didn't have any time for things they considered "baby-ish."

Lewis understood. He had felt that way once—but he knew better now.

"When I was ten, I read fairy tales in secret and would have been ashamed if I had been found doing so," he admitted. "Now that I am fifty, I read them openly. When I became a man I put away childish things, including the fear of childishness and the desire to be very grown-up."

Lewis thought of all the wonderful stories he loved to read as a child and how they impacted his life. It made him sad to think what the children of his day were missing. Yet there weren't many contemporary books he could recommend to them—books that would not merely educate but encourage and inspire them. It was all the more reason Lewis should write stories of his own. "People won't write the books I want, so I have to do it for myself," he concluded.

Lewis's first children's book began with the sentence, "Once there were four children whose names were Peter, Susan, Edmund and Lucy."

Peter was the name of the talking-mouse hero of all the stories he had written as a boy. Lucy was the daughter of Lewis's good friend, Owen Barfield. In addition to naming one of the main characters after her, Lewis decided to dedicate the book to her as well:

My Dear Lucy,

I wrote this story for you, but when I began it I had not realized that girls grow quicker than books. As a result you are already too old for fairy tales, and by the time it is printed and bound you will be older still. But some day you will be old enough to start reading fairy tales again. You can then take it down from some upper shelf, dust it and tell me what you think of it. I shall probably be too deaf to hear, and too old to understand a word you say, but I shall still be

your affectionate Godfather,
C. S. Lewis

In *The Lion, the Witch and the Wardrobe*, the four children are sent to stay at the country home of Professor Kirke. Lewis named the professor for his old tutor, W. T. Kirkpatrick. Kirkpatrick was a gruff but kindhearted man who always insisted his students must learn to use "logic" to carefully think things through. Of course in some ways the character of Professor Kirke was not unlike C. S. Lewis, who had become a professor himself.

While exploring the professor's rambling country home, the children climb into a wardrobe to hide from the no-nonsense housekeeper, Mrs. Macready (Mrs. Moore). Inside the wardrobe, the children discover the magical world of Narnia.

As Lewis created Narnia, he drew on all the imaginary worlds described by the children's authors he loved—Edith Nesbit, Beatrix Potter, and George MacDonald, whom Lewis considered a "master" of fantasy and fairy tale. (MacDonald's best-loved books for children include *The Princess and the Goblin* and *The Princess and Curdie*.) Lewis filled his own world with all the creatures from his favorite fairy tales and legends.

He added bits and pieces from his studies of Roman, Greek, and Hebrew mythology, as well as from medieval literature. And then suddenly he was inspired to weave into the story something infinitely more precious to him—his Christian faith. Through Aslan, Lewis would introduce his readers to the character and person of Jesus Christ—the Son of God, who willingly laid down His life for sinners and rose from the dead in power and glory. (The name "Aslan" comes from the Turkish word for "lion," and in the Bible, Jesus is sometimes referred to as "the Lion of Judah.")

The Lion, the Witch and the Wardrobe was published in 1950, and it became an instant classic—a blockbuster bestseller. By then Lewis had already started working on a second adventure story. In one of his notebooks, he had scribbled:

SEQUEL TO L. W. W. The present tyrants to be Men. Intervening history of Narnia told nominally by a Dwarf

From the pictures in his head and those few words and phrases, he came up with this plot: Sitting at the railway station, returning to school after the holidays, the four Pevensie children find themselves pulled back into Narnia, where it has been a thousand years since they first reigned. They meet a feisty dwarf named Trumpkin who explains to them how dark times have fallen on their former kingdom. Evil men rule the land, and the Talking Beasts have gone into hiding. Young Prince Caspian wants to set things right, but he will need the Pevensies' help to defeat the wicked uncle who has stolen his throne.

The talking-mouse hero that Lewis had imagined in the stories he wrote as a child now made his appearance in Narnia as Reepicheep, the Chief Mouse—one of Caspian's bravest warriors—and one of the most beloved characters in all of the Chronicles. And again, the Great Lion Aslan would prove to be Narnia's Savior—his long-awaited second coming would signal its deliverance.

Lewis thought to call the book *Drawn into Narnia* or *A Horn in Narnia*, but his publisher didn't care for either of those titles. Eventually they settled on *Prince Caspian: The Return to Narnia*, though today it's simply known as *Prince Caspian*. It was first published in 1951.

Lewis began receiving hundreds and hundreds of letters from children who loved his stories about Narnia. They often enclosed drawings of their favorite characters and scenes, which Lewis displayed on his mantelpiece. Young fans often asked him questions about the series: "Why did Reepicheep do this?" "What did it mean when Aslan said that?" And of course, "When is the next book coming out?"

Lewis took the time to answer almost every one. Sometimes he answered their questions directly, but more often than not, he gave them hints instead. A teacher at heart, Lewis liked to challenge children to think things over and see if they couldn't discover the answers for themselves. He even encouraged his young fans to write their own stories about Narnia—to create their own adventures—especially after he had finished the seventh (and final) book of the series. In a letter to a boy named Jonathan, Lewis said:

> *Yours is one of the nicest letters I have had about the Narnian books, and it was very good of you to write it. I'm afraid there will be no more of these stories. But why don't you try writing some Narnian tales? I began to write when I was about your age, and it was the greatest fun. Do try!*
>
> *With all the best wishes,*
>
> > *Yours sincerely,*
> > *C. S. Lewis*

This was, after all, a large part of his purpose in writing the books to begin with. Lewis knew the power of inspiration, imagination, and adventure. Thanks to him—and the Chronicles of Narnia—millions of readers in countries all over the world have discovered it, too.

Peter Pevensie: The oldest of the four British children who first found their way into Narnia. A born leader who now has experience and maturity, Peter quickly resumes his position as Narnia's High King and takes charge in this new adventure—bravely leading Old Narnia into battle to throw off the oppression of wicked King Miraz and restore young Prince Caspian to his rightful place on the throne.

Susan Pevensie: As the oldest sister, she is becoming more grown-up, too—but not in a good way. It takes a long time—and an unexpected encounter with Aslan—for her to let go of her worries and fears, her frustration with her siblings, her preoccupation with practical concerns, and resistance to adventure. Only then is she free to be the queen that Narnia once knew.

Edmund Pevensie: His earlier adventures have changed him forever. Edmund has become a careful, thoughtful young man, full of courage and conviction. This time the former king is the first one to believe in Lucy's claims, no matter how unlikely they seem. And his faith is rewarded.

Lucy Pevensie: The youngest of the four children, she was the first to discover Narnia. Now Queen Lucy is the first to see Aslan and receive his instructions for this new adventure. Always truthful and tenderhearted, she struggles a great deal when her brothers and sister don't believe her story this time, either. But she is beginning to grow up, learning to stand on the courage of her convictions and let nothing hinder her faith.

Trumpkin: A Red Dwarf nicknamed D.L.F. (Dear Little Friend) by the Pevensies, he is a friendly skeptic with a dry sense of humor. He's lived all of his life in hiding and doesn't quite believe in Aslan or the kings and queens—even when they stand before him—but he'll gladly take them to Prince Caspian if there's even a chance it will help Old Narnia find its freedom.

King Miraz: A wicked and ruthless Telmarine, he has killed his own brother and countless nobles of the court in order to take the throne from his nephew, Prince Caspian. Under the rule of Miraz, the few remaining Dwarves, Fauns, Giants, and Talking Beasts who once inhabited Narnia have been forced to live in hiding, longing for deliverance from their evil oppressor.

Prince Caspian: A young Telmarine who loves Old Narnia, he longs to see the kingdom restored to the glory it once knew—in the legendary, almost fairy-tale days of Aslan and the four kings and queens from another world. When his Uncle Miraz threatens to kill him, Caspian runs for his life and discovers that some fairy tales are true.

Doctor Cornelius: Half-human, half-dwarf, he becomes young Prince Caspian's tutor as well as closest friend and advisor. Unbeknownst to King Miraz, Doctor Cornelius teaches Caspian the true history of both Narnia and the Telmarines and warns him of the danger he faces. He also provides the tool Caspian uses to call on Aslan and the kings and queens of old to come to his aid.

Nikabrik: The Black (haired) Dwarf is full of bitterness and anger and hatred toward all mankind. He would kill Prince Caspian if the others would let him; he dismisses the Old Narnians' faith in Aslan and the kings and queens as superstitious nonsense and seeks deliverance for himself and his people from an entirely different source of power.

Trufflehunter: The friendly Badger insists that Trumpkin and Nikabrik join him in coming to Prince Caspian's rescue—offering him shelter as he escapes from his wicked Uncle Miraz. Trufflehunter is a true believer; he holds fast to his faith that Aslan and the four kings and queens will deliver Narnia one day.

Reepicheep: A brave warrior, the Chief Mouse lives for adventure—honor and glory on the field of battle. He fights valiantly in the battle against King Miraz, nearly losing his life and learning an important lesson from Aslan about being overly concerned with pride.

Aslan: The Great Lion, the King of the Beasts, Lord of Narnia and all its Creatures, Son of the Emperor Over the Sea. He is the one "behind all the stories" in the Chronicles of Narnia. And once again it is he who will deliver Narnia, this time from the cruel oppression of the Telmarines.

THE STORY WITHIN THE STORY

"All the same, I do wish. . . . I wish I could have lived in the Old Days.
. . . When everything was quite different. When all the animals could
talk, and there were nice people who lived in the streams and the trees.
Naiads and Dryads they were called. And there were Dwarfs.
And there were lovely little Fauns in all the woods."

—PRINCE CASPIAN

When *Prince Caspian* begins, a thousand years have passed since King Peter and King Edmund and Queen Susan and Queen Lucy ruled from the four thrones at Cair Paravel. Since then, a wicked race of men has conquered the land, silenced the rivers and trees, and killed off most of the Talking Beasts and Dwarves and Fauns and Giants. A remnant remain in hiding, holding on to the faintest hope that somehow Narnia will be delivered from the oppression of the Telmarines—set free and restored to its former glory. Some creatures have grown bitter with centuries of suffering. They begin to doubt that the Great Lion Aslan, Narnia's creator and savior, still exists—if he ever did—or that he cares about their plight. Skeptics say the old stories are nothing more than myths or fairy tales. But there are some who still believe, some who insist that the stories are true—that Aslan *will* come again and Narnia will see a new day. "Now faith is being sure of what we hope for and certain of what we do not see" (Hebrews 11:1).

Reading *Prince Caspian*, one can't help but be reminded of the cycle of oppression and deliverance that God's people experienced repeatedly throughout the Old Testament. Or the four hundred years of silence between the Old Testament and the New Testament when God said nothing, but a faithful remnant clung tightly to the hope of the coming of the Messiah. Then again, it's not unlike the period of persecution that followed Jesus' earthly ministry, when the Roman Empire forced the early church underground. In some ways, it even seems familiar to us today: the wicked flourish, the righteous are oppressed. Scoffers and skeptics call our faith a fairy tale. Jesus said, "Blessed are those who have not seen and yet have believed" (John 20:29).

Prince Caspian appears on the scene like King Josiah in 2 Chronicles 34. The boy king of Judah rejected the wickedness and idolatry of his ancestors and single-handedly turned the nation's clock back. While he was still young, Josiah began to seek God. "He did what was right in the eyes of the LORD" (vv. 2–3). He repaired the temple, restored the priesthood, and rediscovered the Book of the Law. "Josiah removed all the detestable idols from all the territory . . . and he had all who were present in Israel serve the LORD their God. As long as he lived, they did not fail to follow the LORD . . ." (v. 33).

But before Caspian can restore Narnia, he must defeat his evil uncle, the usurper, King Miraz. Caspian rallies Old Narnia around him, and they make a valiant effort to take on the Telmarine army. But they are terribly outnumbered. In a desperate moment, Caspian winds the ancient horn of Queen Susan to call for help. The Pevensie children and Aslan will once again appear in Narnia and "put wrongs to right."

For Peter, Edmund, Susan, and Lucy, their second adventure in Narnia is a lesson in courage: "We also rejoice in our sufferings, because we know that suffering produces perseverance; perseverance, character; and character, hope. And hope does not disappoint us . . ." (Romans 5:3–5). Lucy discovers the cost of discipleship (Matthew 16:24). She and Susan illustrate the story of Mary and Martha in Luke 10:38–42, as Susan allows practical concerns to keep her from experiencing Aslan's presence while Lucy chooses to "sit at his feet."

Prince Caspian also includes powerful illustrations of the following truths: "Our struggle is not against flesh and blood, but against the rulers, against the authorities, against the powers of this dark world and against the spiritual forces of evil in the heavenly realms" (Ephesians 6:12), and "The Lord is not slow in keeping his promise, as some understand slowness. He is patient with you, not wanting anyone to perish, but everyone to come to repentance" (2 Peter 3:9).

These lessons are just a few of the spiritual treasures you will discover as you return to Narnia with *Prince Caspian*.

THE LAND OF NARNIA

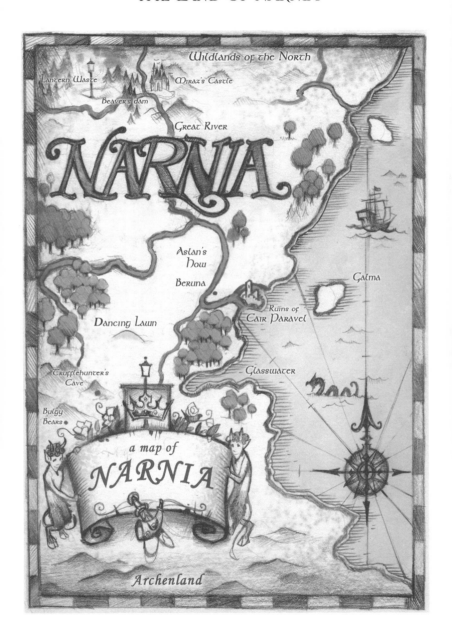

Wildlands of the North

Lantern Waste

Miraz's Castle

Beaver's dam

Great River

NARNIA

Aslan's
How

Beruna

Galma

Dancing Lawn

Ruins of
Cair Paravel

Trufflehunter's
Cave

Glasswater

Bulgy
Bears

a map of
NARNIA

Archenland

A prudent man gives thought to his steps.

1

THE ISLAND

*Let them give thanks to the LORD for his unfailing love . . . he satisfies
the thirsty and fills the hungry with good things.*

PSALM 107:8–9

BIBLICAL PARALLELS AND PRINCIPLES

~ Susan insists that the others put their shoes back on—
and wait to eat their sandwiches. Though her siblings find
it annoying at times, Susan's attention to practical matters
keeps them from making some thoughtless choices or care-
less mistakes. Proverbs 14:15 tells us, "A prudent man gives
thought to his steps."

~ After walking three-quarters of the way around the
island, the children are hot and tired and thirsty. The psalmist compared his spiritual longings to a desperate thirst: "As

the deer pants for streams of water, so my soul pants for you, O God. My soul thirsts for God, for the Living God . . ." (Psalm 42:1–2). Just as cool water from the stream refreshes the children, the psalmist experienced times of refreshing in the presence of the Lord (Psalm 23:1–3a).

DO YOU KNOW?

Though the island is surrounded by water, the children are thirsty; they must find pure, fresh, unsalty water to drink. The book of Exodus tells us that God's people got very thirsty wandering in the desert. How did God provide water for them? (Hint: Read Exodus 17:1–6.)

SCRIPTURES ON HUNGER AND THIRST

- Matthew 5:6
- John 4:13–14
- Revelation 7:16–17

2

THE ANCIENT TREASURE HOUSE

I will remember the deeds of the LORD;
yes, I will remember your miracles of long ago.

PSALM 77:11

BIBLICAL PARALLELS AND PRINCIPLES

~ It's one thing to be cautious—it's another thing to be fearful. As the others grow more and more excited, Susan grows more and more afraid. Her fear is holding her back. The Scripture tells us, "Be strong and courageous. Do not be terrified; do not be discouraged, for the LORD your God will be with you wherever you go" (Joshua 1:9).

~ The children recall their days as kings and queens of Narnia. Though at first they are saddened that those days are gone,

It's important to remember how far we've come!

the happy memories remind them of who they are—who they have been, and all that they have overcome. This gives them courage to face whatever adventure lies ahead. The psalmist said,

These things I remember
as I pour out my soul:
how I used to go with the multitude,
leading the procession to the house of God,
with shouts of joy and thanksgiving
among the festive throng.

Why are you so downcast, O my soul? . . .
Put your hope in God,
for I will yet praise him,
my Savior and my God. (Psalm 42:4–5)

THINK ABOUT IT!

In the ruins of Cair Paravel, the children have uncovered the ancient treasure chamber where, as kings and queens, they kept their most prized possessions. The Scripture says that God is a sure foundation for His people: "a rich store of salvation and wisdom and knowledge." What is the key that unlocks this treasure? (Hint: Read Isaiah 33:5–6.)

SCRIPTURES ON FINDING COURAGE IN THE FACE OF FEAR

- Psalm 46:1–3
- Isaiah 41:10
- Psalm 27:1–6

NEVER FORGET

Oh look! Our coronation rings—do you remember
first wearing this?—Why, this is the little brooch
we all thought was lost—I say, isn't that the armor you wore
in the great tournament in the Lone Islands?—
do you remember the dwarf making that for me?—
do you remember drinking out of that horn?—
do you remember, do you remember?

In the ancient treasure house in the ruins of Cair Paravel,
the four Pevensie children rediscover the treasures of their
past and remember what it was like to be kings and queens
of Narnia. They ruled the kingdom during its "Golden Age."
Though at first the children are sad that those days are gone,
the happy memories remind them of who they are—of who
they have been—and all that they have overcome. They think
of all the trials they've endured, the challenges faced, the battles
fought and won. By the grace of Aslan, they have already accomplished so much! Looking back, the Pevensies find the

strength and courage to move forward. Now they are ready to take on whatever adventure lies ahead.

The psalmist in the Bible had the same experience:

> *These things I remember*
> *as I pour out my soul:*
> *how I used to go with the multitude,*
> *leading the procession to the house of God,*
> *with shouts of joy and thanksgiving*
> *among the festive throng.*
>
> *Why are you so downcast, O my soul? . . .*
> *Put your hope in God,*
> *for I will yet praise him,*
> *my Savior and my God. (Psalm 42:4–5)*

In 1 Peter 2:9, we're reminded that as believers, we have a most high and holy calling—a special purpose, a powerful destiny: "You are a chosen people, a royal priesthood, a holy nation, a people belonging to God, that you may declare the praises of him who called you out of darkness into his wonderful light." What an encouragement, especially for those days we don't feel so special!

In countless other Scriptures, the Bible tells us to always remember—and never forget—what God has done for us, how He has been faithful to protect us and provide for us. After Joshua led the children of Israel across the Jordan River and into the Promised Land, he sent the leaders of the twelve tribes back into the river bed to gather some large stones. "We will use these stones to build a memorial," he said. "In the future your children will ask, 'What do these stones mean to you?' Then you can tell them, 'They remind us that the Jordan River stopped flowing when the Ark of the Lord's Covenant went across.' These stones will stand as a permanent memorial among the people of Israel" (see Joshua 4:6–7). They would always remember how God had demonstrated His mighty power that day.

People all over the world still build memorials today. A memorial is a way to remember something precious, something historic, something vitally important. It's a tradition each of us can carry on in our own hearts, with our own families. And we should, because these are the memories that will help us find the hope and courage and strength we need to see us through dark days.

When God does something miraculous in our lives, we need to take time to build a memorial—to do something special to create a memory of the experience. At the very least, we can stick something on the mirror or refrigerator that will remind us of it. Keep our own "treasures" (symbols or reminders) on our desk or dresser. Write about it in a journal or a scrapbook, talk about it on tape, tell our friends and family, especially our children and grandchildren. If we relive these experiences over and over in our hearts, we'll never forget who we are—or *whose* we are—and all that He has done for us!

God calls us to rescue those who are in danger
and help those who are hurting.

3

THE DWARF

The righteous man is rescued from trouble,
and it comes on the wicked instead.

PROVERBS 11:8

BIBLICAL PARALLELS AND PRINCIPLES

~ Susan and the others come to the aid of the Dwarf immediately. Isaiah 1:17 says, "Seek justice, encourage the oppressed. . . ." And Proverbs 24:11 says, "Rescue those being led away to death; hold back those staggering toward slaughter."

~ All of his life, the Dwarf has been told that the woods on the shore are haunted. The soldiers flee from the island in fear, convinced they have been attacked by "ghosts." The Bible speaks scornfully of people who are "full of superstitions"

(Isaiah 2:6) and "terrified by signs in the sky" (Jeremiah 10:2). Isaiah 8:12–13 tells us,

> *Do not call conspiracy*
> *everything that these people call conspiracy;*
> *do not fear what they fear,*
> *and do not dread it.*
> *The Lord Almighty is the one you are to regard as*
> *holy,*
> *he is the one you are to fear,*
> *he is the one you are to dread.*

SOUND FAMILIAR?

The soldiers are terrified, thinking they've seen a ghost. Even the Dwarf—who has much more courage and common sense—needs a little reassurance. The Bible tells us of some people who thought they had seen a ghost. One of the ways He reassured them that He was real was by eating fish. Do you know who it was? (Hint: Read Luke 24:36–45.)

SCRIPTURES ON THE TERROR OF THE WICKED

- Isaiah 3:11
- Proverbs 10:24
- Proverbs 21:15

4

THE DWARF TELLS OF PRINCE CASPIAN

We did not follow cleverly invented stories when we told you
about the power and coming of our Lord Jesus Christ,
but we were eyewitnesses of his majesty.

2 Peter 1:16

BIBLICAL PARALLELS AND PRINCIPLES

~ The Telmarines have tried to wipe out the memory of Old Narnia and pretend that it never existed. The Bible tells us that godless men "suppress the truth by their wickedness" (Romans 1:18). They have rejected wisdom and reason. "Their thinking became futile and their foolish hearts were darkened. . . . They exchanged the truth of God for a lie" (Romans 1:21, 25). They are no longer capable of understanding what is

God's truth shines brightly through the darkness.

right and true and real, for their hearts have been hardened (Ephesians 4:18).

~ Through his new tutor, Caspian has the opportunity to learn the truth—and to choose a different path than his "grandcestors." This is a choice every believer must make. Ephesians 5 explains, "You were once in darkness, but now you are light in the Lord. Live as children of light . . . in all goodness, righteousness and truth and find out what pleases the Lord. Have nothing to do with the fruitless deeds of darkness, but rather expose them. . . . Be very careful . . . how you live—not as unwise, but as wise, making the most of every opportunity, because the days are evil" (vv. 8–11, 15–16).

DO YOU KNOW?

According to wise, old Doctor Cornelius, the meeting of the stars Tarva and Alambil means "great good for the sad realm of Narnia." Some wise men in the Bible believed that the appearance of a particular star meant that something good was about to happen in Israel. Do you know what it was? (Hint: Read Matthew 2:1–12.)

SCRIPTURES ON KEEPING YOUR MOUTH SHUT

- Proverbs 11:13
- Proverbs 12:23
- Proverbs 13:3

Offer hospitality to one another without grumbling.

5

CASPIAN'S ADVENTURE IN THE MOUNTAINS

Deliver me, O my God, from the hand of the wicked,
from the grasp of evil and cruel men. For you have been my hope,
O Sovereign LORD, my confidence since my youth.

PSALM 71:4–5

BIBLICAL PARALLELS AND PRINCIPLES

~ Over Nikabrik's objections, Trumpkin and Trufflehunter insist on showing kindness to Caspian. The Scripture is full of admonitions such as these: "Share with God's people who are in need. . . ." (Romans 12:13). "The alien living with you must be treated as one of your native-born. Love him as yourself . . ." (Leviticus 19:34). "Offer hospitality to one another without grumbling" (1 Peter 4:9). "Do not forget to entertain strangers, for by so doing some people have entertained angels without knowing it" (Hebrews 13:2).

~ It has been over a thousand years since the Golden Age of Narnia. Nikabrik and Trumpkin have as much trouble believing the stories of Aslan and the kings and queens as some people in our time have trouble believing the Bible. The Scripture tells us, "Faith is being sure of what we hope for and certain of what we do not see" (Hebrews 11:1). Trufflehunter shows the faith Jesus commended in John 20:29, where we read that Jesus said to His disciples, "Because you have seen me, you have believed; blessed are those who have not seen and yet have believed."

DO YOU KNOW?

No matter what the others think, Trufflehunter says that he will be faithful to Aslan and the King. He is a true disciple: "We don't change, we beasts. We don't forget. We hold on." The Bible tells us about Someone who never forgets and never changes and who always remains faithful. Do you know who? (Hint: Read Hebrews 13:8 and 2 Timothy 2:11–13.)

SCRIPTURES ON FAITH

- 2 Corinthians 5:7
- Hebrews 11
- Romans 1:16–17

6

THE PEOPLE THAT LIVED IN HIDING

When the wicked rise to power, people go into hiding;
but when the wicked perish, the righteous thrive.

PROVERBS 28:28

BIBLICAL PARALLELS AND PRINCIPLES

~ Caspian is shocked to realize that the horrible creatures from the old stories are just as real as the nice ones. Many people find it pleasant to believe in the existence of guardian angels. But if we believe the Bible is true, we have to realize that the spirit world is not just inhabited by angels, but also by demons. We have a loving heavenly Father who cares for us; we also have an enemy who seeks to devour us (1 Peter 5:8)! That's why Ephesians 6:11–12 says, "Put on the full

We are not alone in our battle against evil.

armor of God so that you can take your stand against the devil's schemes. For our struggle is not against flesh and blood, but against . . . the powers of this dark world and against the spiritual forces of evil in the heavenly realms."

~ Nikabrik will believe in anyone or anything that will drive the Telmarines out of Narnia. Some of Jesus' followers felt the same way. They would believe in anyone they thought could deliver them from Roman oppression. They wanted to make Jesus their king, but when they realized that He wasn't about to lead a military revolt, they abandoned Him (John 6:15, 66). Scripture tells us that in times of trouble, instead of calling on Him, God's people repeatedly made alliances with heathen nations, worshiped false gods, and appealed to evil spirits for help (Isaiah 30:1–2; 31:1). The results were always disastrous.

DO YOU KNOW?

To his delight, Caspian discovers that there are many Old Narnians still living—they've just been in hiding. During the reign of a wicked king, a prophet complained that he was the only servant of God still living in the land—until God told him that there were seven thousand others! Many of them were just in hiding. Do you remember the prophet's name? (Hint: Read 1 Kings 19:14–18; see also 1 Kings 18:4.)

SCRIPTURES ON HIDING IN GOD

- Psalm 17:6–9
- Psalm 32:7
- Psalm 143:9

NOT THE ONLY ONE

"All the same, I do wish . . . I wish I could have lived
in the Old Days . . . when everything was quite different.
When all the animals could talk, and there were nice people
who lived in the streams and the trees.
Naiads and Dryads they were called. And there were Dwarfs.
And there were lovely little Fauns in all the woods. . . ."
"That's all nonsense . . ." said the King sternly.
"You're getting too old for that sort of stuff."

What Caspian is really wishing for is something better, something truer, something deeper than what he has known. Somehow instinctively he understands that his world is not as it should be—or as it once was—and he longs to see it restored to its former glory. But as a child, Caspian learns the hard way not to share his longings out loud. Those around him don't feel the same way at all. When his nurse is dismissed for "filling his head with nonsense," Caspian feels very much alone.

Some of us can relate. Our values are so different from those of the world we live in, our hopes and dreams so out of sync with the rest of society. Our faith is routinely dismissed by others as nothing more than a fairy tale. We feel so alone.

The Bible tells us that the prophet Elijah once complained that he was the only servant of God still living in the land. It seemed like all others had turned their backs on God and abandoned their faith. Elijah was the only one left—or so he thought. But then God told him there were seven thousand others that the prophet knew nothing about—courageous men and women who were living out their faith day by day, even in the face of overwhelming opposition (1 Kings 18:4; 19:14–18).

Elijah wasn't the only one left—and neither was Prince Caspian. Caspian's new tutor, Doctor Cornelius, assures him that there are others who feel the way he does. After a daring midnight escape from his uncle's castle, Caspian finds himself rescued by two dwarfs, Trumpkin and Nikabrik, and Trufflehunter, a talking badger. To Caspian's delight, he discovers that there are many of these Old Narnians still living—they've just been in hiding. These people share his faith, his hopes, his dreams. He is not alone.

And neither are we. There are people all over the world who share our values, our faith, our hopes, and our dreams. People who are committed to what they believe in, who are willing to take a stand for what is good and right and true (1 Peter 5:8–10). For all the headline-grabbing evil and immorality that goes on in our world today, there are still those who daily practice acts of kindness and generosity, heroism and self-sacrifice.

We can be proud to be counted among them.

7

OLD NARNIA IN DANGER

*The night is nearly over; the day is almost here. So let us put aside
the deeds of darkness and put on the armor of light.*

ROMANS 13:12

BIBLICAL PARALLELS AND PRINCIPLES

~ At the council of war, Caspian listens to the wisdom
and guidance of Doctor Cornelius, Glenstorm, Trufflehunter,
and the others. Proverbs 20:18 says, "Make plans by seeking
advice; if you wage war, obtain guidance." And Proverbs 11:14
observes, "For lack of guidance a nation falls, but many advisors make victory sure."

~ Caspian decides to use Queen Susan's horn to summon
help. In the Scriptures, the sound of the horn called soldiers

Many advisors make victory sure!

to battle. It was a cry for help. The horn also symbolized power and strength and deliverance (see 2 Samuel 22:3; Psalm 89:16–17, 24; Psalm 112:9). Zechariah prophesied about the coming of the Messiah (Jesus) in Luke 1:68–75: "Praise be to the Lord. . . . He has raised up a horn of salvation for us . . . to rescue us from the hand of our enemies, and to enable us to serve him without fear in holiness and righteousness before him all our days."

SOUND FAMILIAR?

Aslan's How is a sacred memorial mound, built like a tomb over the ruins of the Stone Table. Inside are tunnels and caves, all lined with stones that form mosaics. Many feature a lion or some other ancient and mysterious symbol. When the early church suffered persecution from the Roman emperors, they went underground—building miles of caves and tunnels and passages called catacombs. They used the catacombs as a secret refuge, a place to meet for worship and prayer, and a place to bury their loved ones. Archaeologists have found these tunnels lined with mosaics depicting scenes from the life of Christ, as well as doves, fish, and other Christian symbols.

SCRIPTURES ON PERSEVERING IN BATTLE

- Romans 8:31–37
- Psalm 18:32–39
- 1 Timothy 6:12

God has given each of us special skills and talents.

8

How They Left the Island

Be merciful to those who doubt.

Jude 22

BIBLICAL PARALLELS AND PRINCIPLES

~ The children realize that they did not stumble into Narnia by accident—they have been called. The Bible tells us all believers are called by God to fulfill His plans and purposes here on earth: "You are a chosen people, a royal priesthood, a holy nation, a people belonging to God, that you may declare the praises of him who called you out of darkness into his wonderful light" (1 Peter 2:9).

~ Trumpkin can't see how four children could possibly help Narnia. First Corinthians 1:26–27 says, "Brothers, think of what you were when you were called. Not many of you were wise by human standards; not many were influential; not many were of noble birth. But God chose the foolish things of the world to shame the wise; God chose the weak things of the world to shame the strong."

~ Each of the children takes turns demonstrating his or her abilities and talents—and the unique gifts Aslan has given him or her. The Bible tells us that all believers have received gifts from God. These gifts include wisdom, knowledge, administration, faith, healing, miracles, prophecy, and discernment (1 Corinthians 12:8–11, 28–31). We are to use our gifts to help one another, strengthen one another, and build up the body of Christ. "If one part suffers, every part suffers with it; if one part is honored, every part rejoices with it" (1 Corinthians 12:26).

DO YOU KNOW?

Trumpkin says he believes the children, but he doesn't really understand who they are and what they are able to do. Some of Jesus' disciples had the same problem. How did Jesus demonstrate His power to them? (Hint: Read Matthew 14:22–33.)

SCRIPTURES ON DOUBT

- Matthew 13:57–58
- James 1:5–8
- Matthew 21:18–22

9

WHAT LUCY SAW

Let your eyes look straight ahead, fix your gaze directly before you.
Make level paths for your feet and take only ways that are firm.

PROVERBS 4:25–26

BIBLICAL PARALLELS AND PRINCIPLES

~ Seeing the wild bear, Lucy begins to wonder what might happen if, here in our world, "men started going wild inside." Scripture tells us that is exactly what has happened—and will continue to happen as human history draws to a close: "There will be terrible times in the last days. People will be . . . abusive . . . unholy . . . without self-control, brutal . . . treacherous, rash, conceited, lovers of pleasure rather than lovers of God" (2 Timothy 3:1–4). Romans 1:28–29 says, "Furthermore, since they did not think it worthwhile to retain the knowledge

Others may not see what we see.

of God, he gave them over to a depraved mind, to do what ought not to be done. They have become filled with every kind of wickedness, evil, greed and depravity. . . ." (See also Romans 1:18–32; Jude 10.)

~ Lucy is heartbroken that no one believes her. They all insist that she can't have seen Aslan. A young woman named Mary Magdalene was the first one to see Jesus after His death and resurrection. "She went and told those who had been with him. . . . When they heard that Jesus was alive and that she had seen him, they did not believe it" (Mark 16:10–11; see also Luke 24:10–11).

DO YOU KNOW?

In *The Lion, the Witch and the Wardrobe*, Edmund teased Lucy mercilessly about her "imaginary" country—only to discover that her story was true. He has learned from his experience. Where he had been proud and arrogant, he is now humble and thoughtful. What does the Bible say comes with humility? (Hint: Read Proverbs 11:2.)

SCRIPTURES ON FINDING THE RIGHT PATH

- Psalm 16:11
- Proverbs 3:5–6
- Psalm 23:1–4

WILD INSIDE

*Lucy was knocked down and winded, hearing the twang
of a bowstring as she fell. When she was able to take notice of things
again, she saw a great grim-looking gray bear lying dead
with Trumpkin's arrow in its side. . . .*
"I—I left it too late," said Susan, in an embarrassed voice.
*"I was so afraid it might be, you know—one of our kind of bears,
a talking bear." She hated killing things.*
*"That's the trouble of it," said Trumpkin, "when most of the beasts
have gone enemy and gone dumb, but there are still some of the other
kind left. You never know, and you daren't wait to see."*

Deep in the woods, Lucy and the others have come face to face with a "lapsed" bear—a bear who used to be a talking beast but rejected the gift of speech and reason given to him by his Creator (Aslan) only to return to the wild. Trumpkin says that sadly, many other animals in Narnia have done the same. The children realize that it's difficult to tell the difference between a friendly, talking beast and a fierce, wild one just by looking at them. How do you know if you're meeting friend or foe? Then Lucy has a horrid thought:

"Wouldn't it be dreadful if some day in our own world . . . men started going wild inside, like the animals here, and still looked like men, so that you'd never know which were which?"

Susan quickly dismisses the idea, but the Bible tells us that is exactly what *has* happened—and will continue to happen as human history draws to a close. "There will be terrible times in the last days. People will be lovers of themselves, lovers of money, boastful, proud, abusive, disobedient to their parents, ungrateful, unholy, without love, unforgiving, slanderous, without self-control, brutal, not lovers of the good, treacherous, rash, conceited, lovers of pleasure rather than lovers of God" (2 Timothy 3:1–4).

Romans 1:28–29 explains, "Furthermore, since they did not think it worthwhile to retain the knowledge of God, he gave them over to a depraved mind to do what ought not to be done. They have become filled with every kind of wickedness, evil, greed, and depravity. . . ."

The scary thing is that these people walk among us every day, though we don't always recognize them. In some cases, it can be downright difficult—if not impossible—to tell just by looking at the outside who is dangerous and which people have gone "wild inside." If we're not careful, we can be tricked and trapped and taken advantage of. We can find ourselves in all kinds of trouble, completely at the mercy of people who are merciless.

That's why Scripture warns us to be alert and stay on our guard. Jesus said, "I am sending you out like sheep among wolves. . . ." He added, "Be as shrewd [or wary] as snakes and as innocent[or gentle] as doves" (Matthew 10:16).

Every day, we need to keep our eyes open. We need to ask God for His guidance and protection as we make our way through an increasingly wicked world. The good news is that He has promised to walk through it with us and to never leave us or forsake us. And greater is He who is in us than he who is in the world (1 John 4:4).

Some things are much bigger than they appear.

10

THE RETURN OF THE LION

Seek the LORD while he may be found; call on him while he is near.

ISAIAH 55:6

BIBLICAL PARALLELS AND PRINCIPLES

~ Aslan says he seems bigger to Lucy because she is older. Usually the opposite is true: As we grow bigger, we discover the things that seemed so big to us before are actually *smaller* than we remember them. Not so with God. The bigger we get, the more we realize how truly big He is, how small we are, and how much we still have to learn. In Ephesians 3:17–19, the Apostle Paul said, "I pray that you, being rooted and established in love, may have power, together with all the saints, to grasp how wide and long and high and deep is the love of Christ . . . that you may be filled to the measure of all the fullness of God."

~ Lucy feels sorry for herself at the thought of the unpleasant task before her. But Aslan reminds her that "it has been hard for us all in Narnia before now." Others have suffered so much more. In 1 Peter 5:9, battle-weary believers are encouraged to keep resisting the devil and stand firm in their faith, "because you know that your brothers throughout the world are undergoing the same kind of sufferings."

~ Aslan tells Lucy that if the others don't believe her, it doesn't matter: "You at least must follow me alone." Throughout His earthly ministry, Jesus called people to leave their homes, their families, their businesses—to sacrifice everything—to follow Him. He warned His disciples that their own brothers and sisters would turn against them because of Him (Luke 12:51–53). When the disciples asked what God would require of others, Jesus replied, "What is that to you? You must follow Me" (John 21:22).

DO YOU KNOW?

Lucy has a very special relationship with Aslan. Because she follows him whole-heartedly, she draws closer to him and learns to know him better than some of the others do. One of Jesus' disciples was especially close to His heart. Do you remember who? (Hint: Read John 13:22–25; 21:24. Four books of the New Testament bear his name.)

SCRIPTURES ON THE DIFFERENCE BETWEEN GOD'S WAYS AND OUR OWN

- Isaiah 55:8–9
- 1 Corinthians 2:10–14
- Romans 11:33–36

YOU MUST FOLLOW ME

"Now, child," said Aslan, . . . "I will wait here.
Go and wake the others and tell them to follow. If they will not,
then you at least must follow me alone. . . ."
When the whole party was finally awake Lucy had to tell her story
for the fourth time. The blank silence which followed
it was as discouraging as anything could be. . . .
"And I do hope," said Lucy in a tremulous voice, "that you will all
come with me. Because—because I'll have to go with him
whether anyone else does or not."

Lucy is faced with an enormous challenge, an incredibly difficult task. For some reason, she is the only one who can see the Great Lion. Yet somehow, she must convince everyone else to follow her, to follow Him, and to continue their journey in the middle of the night, taking a completely different direction than the one they had chosen. The others insist that Lucy is imagining things. It's all in her head! They complain bitterly at the interruption of their sleep. They have nothing but harsh words for Lucy.

When we choose to follow God's leading, we will often find ourselves in similar situations—faced with ridicule and rejection, even persecution. Others won't believe us, won't understand us, won't agree with the direction we've taken or the decisions we've made. Sometimes that rejection or persecution will come from our closest friends and family. It can be so hard to take! But the Bible tells us we're not alone. Someone else has faced what we face. He knows all about our heartache. He truly feels our pain. First Peter 2:21 explains, "This suffering is all part of what God has called you to. Christ, who suffered for you, is your example. Follow in His steps" (NLT).

No one said it would be easy. Whenever the going gets tough, we will find ourselves tempted to give in and give up. But if we have put our faith in Jesus—if we have given our hearts and lives to Him—then the truth is that we have already made our choice. Remember the words of the old chorus: "I Have Decided to Follow Jesus." The fourth verse boldly proclaims: "Though none go with me, still I will follow; no turning back, no turning back."

When we faithfully follow God's leading—no matter what the cost—we experience the precious peace and comfort and joy that comes from an intimate friendship with Him. We reap the blessings and rewards of obedience:

> *Trust in the LORD with all your heart*
> *and lean not on your own understanding;*
> *in all your ways acknowledge him,*
> *and he will make your paths straight.*
> *(Proverbs 3:5–6)*

And sometimes we find—as Lucy did—that by our example, we give others the courage to follow Him, too.

11

THE LION ROARS

The hour has come for you to wake up from your slumber,
because our salvation is nearer now than when we first believed.

ROMANS 13:11

BIBLICAL PARALLELS AND PRINCIPLES

~ Regardless of what the others say or do, Lucy knows she must obey Aslan—she must follow him. First Peter 3:14–16 tells us how we should respond to similar situations in our lives: "Even if you should suffer for what is right, you are blessed. 'Do not fear what they fear; do not be frightened.' But in your hearts set apart Christ as Lord. Always be prepared to give an answer to everyone who asks you to give the reason for the hope that you have. But do this with gentleness and respect, keeping a clear

Some things are true, whether we believe them or not!

conscience, so that those who speak maliciously against your good behavior in Christ may be ashamed of their slander."

~ Lucy forgot everything—her fears and her frustrations with Susan—when she "fixed her eyes on Aslan." Hebrews 12:1–3 says, "Since we are surrounded by such a great cloud of witnesses, let us throw off everything that hinders and the sin that so easily entangles, and let us run with perseverance the race marked out for us. Let us fix our eyes on Jesus, the author and perfecter of our faith, who for the joy set before him endured the cross, scorning its shame, and sat down at the right hand of the throne of God. Consider him who endured such opposition from sinful men, so that you will not grow weary and lose heart."

~ Aslan leads the children right through the gorge—along secret paths and hidden ledges they failed to discover on their own. In Isaiah 42:16, God says, "I will lead the blind by ways they have not known, along unfamiliar paths I will guide them; I will turn the darkness into light before them and make the rough places smooth. These are the things I will do; I will not forsake them."

~ Aslan tells Susan that she has "listened to [her] fears." In her guilt and shame, she can barely face him. First John 3:19–20 reminds us to focus on God's love for us, as expressed by Jesus' death on the cross: "This then is how . . . we set our hearts at rest in his presence whenever our hearts condemn us. For God is greater than our hearts, and he knows every-thing." Aslan breathes on Susan, just as Jesus breathed on His frightened disciples (John 20:22), and reassures her of his love.

First John 4:18 tells us, "There is no fear in love, but perfect love casts out fear" (ESV).

~ Aslan greets Edmund with the words, "Well done." In Matthew 25:21, Jesus described how God responds to our obedience to Him: "Well done, good and faithful servant! You have been faithful with a few things; I will put you in charge of many things. Come and share your master's happiness!"

~ In spite of their lack of sleep, Peter and Edmund show no signs of weariness. Being in Aslan's presence has refreshed them. Isaiah 40:29–31 tells us that God "gives strength to the weary and increases the power of the weak. Even youths grow tired and weary, and young men stumble and fall; but those who hope in the LORD will renew their strength. They will soar on wings like eagles; they will run and not grow weary, they will walk and not be faint."

DO YOU KNOW?

Susan and Lucy once again witness Aslan's miraculous deliverance of Narnia. They participate in a fantastic celebration—singing, dancing, and feasting. Do you know who or what the Bible says will enjoy a "continual feast"? (Hint: Read Proverbs 15:15.)

SCRIPTURES ON PERSEVERING IN TIMES OF TESTING

- Philippians 3:7–14
- James 1:2–4
- Hebrews 12:4–13

FEAR OR FAITH

Then, after an awful pause, the deep voice said, "Susan."
Susan made no answer but the others thought she was crying.
"You have listened to fears, child," said Aslan.

Susan had refused to believe that Aslan was leading them through the rocky gorge, because she couldn't see him—though she later admitted that in her heart, she knew he was there. She didn't want to believe, because she was afraid of what it would mean. She was afraid that if she followed Aslan, he would take her where she didn't want to go. Susan was so miserable. All she could think about was escaping the woods—and what if Aslan led them deeper in? But of course, the opposite was true. Aslan had come to lead them out. Now, in her guilt and shame, Susan can barely face the Great Lion.

Many of us can relate. At times, we all let fear rule our hearts instead of faith. We're afraid things won't turn out the way we want them to, so we take them into our own hands instead of trusting them to God. We act out of a desire to protect ourselves from difficult or uncomfortable circumstances, rather than a commitment to do what is right. And we make such a mess of things. Later, when we're confronted with the sinful attitudes behind our actions, we feel guilty and ashamed. We know better. We should have trusted God with this. Why didn't we run to Him—instead of running *from* Him?

We know He must be disappointed in us; we're so disappointed in ourselves. We can't even face Him.

But in C. S. Lewis's story, Aslan doesn't punish Susan or put her down. He comforts her. He breathes on her, just as Jesus breathed on His frightened disciples (John 20:22), and reassures her of his love.

The Bible says that's what Jesus wants to do for us. The Scriptures tell us over and over to remember how much God loves us, even as we repent of our sinful behavior. "This then is how . . . we set our hearts at rest in his presence whenever our hearts condemn us. For God is greater than our hearts, and he knows everything." (1 John 3:19–20). He understands our human weakness, our fears, our frailty. He loves us anyway. And as 1 John 4:18 explains, "There is no fear in love, but perfect love casts out fear" (ESV).

Lucy experienced the power of this truth earlier in their adventures. She found that she forgot everything—all of her fears and her frustrations—when she "fixed her eyes on Aslan." As she looked at him, everything else faded away. And she found the courage to joyfully do everything he asked of her.

It can be that way for you and me today. Hebrews 12:1–3 says, "Since we are surrounded by such a great cloud of witnesses, let us throw off everything that hinders and the sin that so easily entangles, and let us run with perseverance the race marked out for us. Let us fix our eyes on Jesus, the author and perfecter of our faith, who for the joy set before him endured the cross, scorning its shame, and sat down at the right hand of the throne of God. Consider him who endured such opposition from sinful men, so that you will not grow weary and lose heart."

When we look at Jesus, we find that our fears and frustrations melt away. When we think about what He suffered for us, our sufferings pale in comparison. When we remember who He really is and all that He has done for us, we realize that He is more than able to care for us—to protect us and provide for us, to lead us and guide us—today.

We cannot make friends with the enemies of God.

12

SORCERY AND SUDDEN VENGEANCE

Woe to those who call evil good and good evil,
who put darkness for light and light for darkness. . . .

ISAIAH 5:20

BIBLICAL PARALLELS AND PRINCIPLES

~ Nikabrik insists that no help has come, but Trufflehunter says prophetically, "It may be even now at the door." The badger's faith is like that of the psalmist who said, "I am still confident of this: I will see the goodness of the LORD in the land of the living" (Psalm 27:13). Isaiah 30:18 tells us, "The LORD longs to be gracious to you; he rises to show you compassion. For the LORD is a God of justice. Blessed are all who wait for him!"

~ Nikabrik questions the truth of the old stories, suggesting that Aslan never rose from the dead and that much of what Narnians have believed is nothing more than myth or fairy tale. Since the cross, unbelievers have brought those same accusations against Christians. Matthew 28:11–15 tells us how the soldiers who witnessed Jesus' resurrection conspired to say that He did not rise from the dead, that His disciples merely stole His body: "And this story has been widely circulated . . . to this day." But the Apostle Peter insisted, "We did not follow cleverly invented stories when we told you about the power and coming of our Lord Jesus Christ, but we were eyewitnesses of his majesty" (2 Peter 1:16).

~ When Nikabrik suggests that they summon the White Witch, Caspian responds with righteous anger. In the Scriptures, God absolutely forbids necromancy—the attempt to contact the spirits of the dead. Isaiah 8:19 says, "When men tell you to consult mediums and spiritists, who whisper and mutter, should not a people inquire of their God? Why consult with the dead on behalf of the living?" Deuteronomy 18:10–12 tells us, "Anyone who does these things is detestable to the LORD."

~ Though he had never seen Aslan himself, and though stories of the kings and queens were a thousand years old, still Trufflehunter persisted in his faith. In 1 Peter 1:8–9, the apostle Peter speaks to those of us who did not have the opportunity to walk with Jesus as he and the other disciples did and yet still believe. "Though you have not seen him, you love him; and even though you do not see him now, you believe in him and are filled with an inexpressible and glorious joy, for you are receiving the goal of your faith, the salvation of your souls." One day, like Trufflehunter, we will have the privilege of meeting the One in whom we have believed—the King of kings—face to face.

DO YOU KNOW?

For years, Nikabrik allowed hatred and bitterness to fill his heart, until it consumed him. What does the Bible tell us to do with those emotions? (Hint: Read Ephesians 4:31–5:2.)

SCRIPTURES ON WAITING FOR GOD'S DELIVERANCE

- Psalm 33:20–22
- Lamentations 3:22–26
- Romans 8:18–25

MORE THAN A FAIRY TALE

"You, you great clerk, you master magician, you know-all;
are you still asking us to hang our hopes on Aslan
and King Peter and all the rest of it?" . . .
"The help will come," said Trufflehunter. . . . *"Have patience.* . . .
The help will come. It may be even now at the door."

In the days of Prince Caspian, a small remnant of Narnian creatures eagerly await deliverance from the Telmarines—the foreign oppressors who conquered their ancestors. These true believers have been driven underground for hundreds of years during the occupation of their homeland. Some begin to lose hope that they will ever be free again. When their savior, the Great Lion Aslan does not appear immediately in response to their desperate appeals, Nikabrik the Dwarf questions the truth of the old stories. A skeptic through and through, he suggests that perhaps Aslan never really rose from the dead all those years ago—and that much of what the Narnians have believed is nothing more than myth or fairy tale.

You know, ever since the cross, unbelievers have brought those same accusations against Christians. It started way back then. Matthew 28:11–15 tells us that the Roman soldiers who witnessed Jesus' resurrection conspired together to say that He did not rise from the dead—that His disciples had secretly stolen His body and hidden it away: "And this story has been widely circulated . . . to this day." But the Apostle Peter insists, "We did not follow cleverly invented stories when we told you about the power and coming of our Lord Jesus Christ, but we were eyewitnesses of his majesty" (2 Peter 1:16). Peter says he was there when it happened. He knows the truth, no matter what anyone else says.

It's been thousands of years since the days of Jesus' earthly ministry. And sometimes—even to those of us who are Christians—the events at the foundation of our faith seem like fairy tales, things that happened "once upon a time" and "far, far away." They are hard to imagine and even harder to believe.

But they couldn't be more true. Somehow we've got to hold onto our faith. We can't give in to doubt and despair. For to those of us who did not have the opportunity to walk with Jesus, as Peter and the other disciples did, and yet still believe, Peter said, "Though you have not seen him, you love him; and even though you do not see him now, you believe in him and are filled with an inexpressible and glorious joy, for you are receiving the goal of your faith, the salvation of your souls." (1 Peter 1:8–9).

One day, just like the faithful creatures in C. S. Lewis's story, we will have the privilege of meeting the One in whom we have believed—face to face. We'll walk with Him and talk with Him, just as those first disciples did. Those precious moments will be worth everything we've been through—all of the hardship, all of the work, all of the wait.

James 1:12 tells us our faithfulness will be rewarded. "Blessed is the man who perseveres under trial, because when he has stood the test, he will receive the crown of life that God has promised to those who love him." And that's no fairy tale.

The advice of the wicked is deceitful.

13

THE HIGH KING IN COMMAND

The integrity of the upright guides them,
but the unfaithful are destroyed by their duplicity.

PROVERBS 11:3

BIBLICAL PARALLELS AND PRINCIPLES

~ Peter observes that Aslan acts "in his time . . . not ours." The Scripture often uses phrases such as "in the fullness of time" or "at the appointed time" to indicate that everything happens just as God ordains—according to His plan and His timetable. "With the Lord a day is like a thousand years, and a thousand years are like a day" (2 Peter 3:8). We don't always understand the delay, but 2 Peter 3:9 assures us that "the Lord is not slow in keeping his promise, as some understand slowness. He is patient. . . ." According to Ecclesiastes 3:11, "He has made everything beautiful in its time. . . ."

~ A "kind of greatness" has hung about Edmund since his encounter with Aslan. The Bible tells us that after Moses met with God on Mount Sinai, his face shone so brightly that he had to wear a veil (Exodus 34:29–33). Second Corinthians 3:18 says that now all believers, with unveiled faces, "reflect the Lord's glory." Acts 4:13 tells us that the disciples were put on trial, and when the people "saw the courage of Peter and John and realized that they were unschooled, ordinary men, they were astonished and they took note that these men had been with Jesus."

~ Miraz has surrounded himself with evil men—the kind who would support his murderous plans and aid him in his treachery. But he is foolish to make such men his counselors. Proverbs 12:5 warns, "The advice of the wicked is deceitful." Proverbs 26:24–25 explains, "A malicious man disguises himself with his lips, but in his heart he harbors deceit. Though his speech is charming, do not believe him, for seven abominations fill his heart."

SOUND FAMILIAR?

Peter begins his challenge to Miraz by referring to his position as High King "by the gift of Aslan." (The phrase at once asserts his authority: Aslan appointed him and put him in charge. At the same time, it is a humble acknowledgement that his power comes from Aslan and not from himself.) One of the early church leaders began nearly all of his letters the same way, referring to himself as an apostle appointed by Jesus Christ. Do you know who? (Hint: Read Galatians 1:1; see also Romans 1:1; 1 and 2 Corinthians 1:1; Ephesians 1:1; Colossians 1:1; 1 and 2 Timothy 1:1; and Titus 1:1.)

SCRIPTURES ON THE WAYS OF THE WISE

- Proverbs 14:29
- Proverbs 17:27
- Proverbs 19:11

*The Lord will redeem them from the hand
of those stronger than they.*

14

HOW ALL WERE VERY BUSY

When justice is done, it brings joy to the righteous
but terror to evildoers.

PROVERBS 21:15

BIBLICAL PARALLELS AND PRINCIPLES

~ Almost before the Narnians are "really warmed to their work," the Telmarines are defeated. In Exodus 23:27, God promised, "I will send my terror ahead of you and throw into confusion every nation you encounter. I will make all your enemies turn their backs and run."

~ Once again Aslan brings deliverance to Narnia, setting the captives free (compare Isaiah 61:1). Jeremiah 31:11–13 describes how God will deliver His people: "For the LORD will

. . . redeem them from the hand of those stronger than they. They will come and shout for joy on the heights of Zion; they will rejoice in the bounty of the LORD—the grain, the new wine and the oil, the young of the flocks and herds. They will be like a well-watered garden, and they will sorrow no more. Then maidens will dance and be glad, young men and old as well. I will turn their mourning into gladness; I will give them comfort and joy instead of sorrow."

~ Aslan not only delivers Old Narnia, but he rescues Telmarines whose hearts are tender toward him. Jesus made it clear that He did not come to save only one race or people (John 10:16; 1 John 2:2). Revelation 5:9 tells us that with His blood, He has purchased or redeemed men "from every tribe and language and people and nation." In Revelation 3:20, Jesus issued an open invitation: "Here I am! I stand at the door and knock. If anyone hears my voice and opens the door, I will come in. . . ."

SOUND FAMILIAR?

Bacchus hands Caspian's old nurse a pitcher of water from the well. Upon tasting it, she discovers that it has been turned to wine! Someone in the Bible offered the thirsty "a spring of water welling up into eternal life," and His first miracle was turning water into wine. Do you know who it was? (Hint: Read John 4:13–14 and John 2:7–11.)

SCRIPTURES ON CELEBRATING GOD'S VICTORY

- Exodus 15:1–13
- Psalm 148
- Revelation 11:17–18

For the sake of his friends, He healed the man.

15

ASLAN MAKES A DOOR IN THE AIR

*This day I call heaven and earth as witnesses . . . that I have set before
you life and death, blessings and curses. Now choose life, so that you
and your children may live and that you may love the LORD your God,
listen to his voice, and hold fast to him. For the LORD is your life. . . .*

DEUTERONOMY 30:19–20

BIBLICAL PARALLELS AND PRINCIPLES

~ Aslan tells Caspian that if he had felt himself sufficient,
it would have been proof that he was not. Romans 12:3 tells
us, "Do not think of yourselves more highly than you ought
. . ." And 1 Corinthians 10:12 says, "If you think you are
standing firm, be careful that you don't fall!" The apostle Paul
urged believers to "put no confidence in the flesh" (Philip-

pians 3:3). Instead, we should recognize our human frailty and our total dependence on God. "He [God] said to me, 'My grace is sufficient for you, for my power is made perfect in weakness.' Therefore I will boast all the more gladly about my weaknesses, so that Christ's power might rest on me" (2 Corinthians 12:9).

~ Reepicheep's friends bring him to Aslan for healing. In Luke 5:18–26 some friends brought a paralyzed man to Jesus. When they couldn't get in at the door because of the crowds, they lowered him through the roof on a mat. Jesus was moved when He "saw their faith." For the sake of his friends, He healed the man.

~ Lucy has a special relationship with Aslan; she loves him wholeheartedly and serves him faithfully. At the feast, she is "sitting close" to him—a picture of devotion. The Scriptures describe the same devotion in Mary of Bethany, who sat at Jesus' feet (Luke 10:39), and John the Beloved, who leaned back against Jesus at the Last Supper (John 13:25).

~ Aslan "feasted the Narnians" all day and all night. Throughout His earthly ministry, Jesus fed His disciples, sometimes four or five thousand at a time (Matthew 14:13–21; 15:29–38)! In His parables, He often used banquets and feasts to describe the kingdom of God (Matthew 22:1–14; Luke 14:15–23). Jesus promised that one day all believers would join Him for a magnificent celebration in Heaven—"the wedding supper of the Lamb" (Revelation 19:9).

~ Caspian learns that being a Son of Adam or Daughter of Eve is both an honor and shame. It is an honor to be unique among all Creation: "created . . . in the image of God" (Genesis 1:27; see also 2:7). But it is a shame to be responsible for bringing sin and death into the world. "Through the disobedience of one man, the many were made sinners" (Romans 5:19).

SOUND FAMILIAR?

Susan and Lucy are very similar to two sisters in the Bible. One—like Susan—was focused on "practical things," while the other—like Lucy—focused on "spiritual things." Do you remember the sisters' names? (Hint: Read Luke 10:38–42.)

SCRIPTURES ON LIFE-CHANGING CHOICES

- Joshua 24:14–15
- John 3:16–18
- John 15:16

READY OR NOT

Then Peter, leading Caspian, forced his way
through the crowd of animals.
"This is Caspian, Sir," he said.
And Caspian knelt and kissed the Lion's paw.
"Welcome, Prince," said Aslan. "Do you feel yourself sufficient
to take up the Kingship of Narnia?"
"I—I don't think I do, Sir," said Caspian. "I'm only a kid."
"Good," said Aslan. "If you had felt yourself sufficient,
it would have been proof that you were not."

Caspian isn't sure he's ready to be King of Narnia—and Aslan says that means he is! If the young prince had been more confident about taking the throne, it would have revealed how little he understood both the privilege and the responsibility of leading a nation. But in his humility, Caspian reveals his maturity. He knows it's more than he can handle, and he's willing to admit it. That means he is also willing to ask for help. Caspian is willing to look to Aslan, Narnia's Creator and its Savior, for the wisdom and guidance and strength he needs to rule his people. Aslan is pleased.

The Bible tells us one of Israel's kings showed the same maturity as Caspian. Solomon wasn't sure that he was ready to be king. He faced a daunting task, trying to follow in the footsteps of his father David, the greatest king Israel would ever know. One night, soon after Solomon's coronation, God appeared to him in a dream and said, "Ask for whatever you want me to give you" (1 Kings 3:5).

It was a staggering offer! Can you imagine? What might the young king have asked for? What do most kings want? Power, prestige, prosperity, peace, the destruction of their enemies, riches beyond measure. But Solomon asked for none of these things. Instead, he humbly confessed that he felt unequal to the task of ruling a great nation. He was young and inexperienced. But he desperately wanted to do what was right in the eyes of the Lord and to take good care of His people. Solomon said, "O LORD my God, you have made your servant king in place of my father David. But I am only a little child and do not know how to carry out my duties. . . . So give your servant a discerning heart to govern your people and to distinguish between right and wrong . . ." (1 Kings 3:7, 9).

Solomon asked for wisdom: a discerning or understanding heart. Scripture tells us that God was pleased with this request—so pleased that He gave him everything he asked for and much, much more.

We aren't all called to rule countries and kingdoms, but we all have responsibilities and relationships that challenge us. We all have times when we feel overwhelmed by the situations and circumstances we face. Often these things are way beyond our wisdom and experience—far too much for us to handle. We're in over our heads. But God has put us where we are for a reason; He has placed us in this particular position for a purpose.

And James 1:5 assures us, "If any of you lacks wisdom, he should ask God, who gives generously to all without finding fault, and it will be given to him."

Whether we feel ready or not, if we ask God, He will give us all the wisdom and strength we need to accomplish great things in His name.

Continuing the Adventure

There are many ways you can continue your own adventures in Narnia—activities, crafts, and projects that will help you celebrate your favorite moments in the story. Here are just a few.

APPLES, APPLES, AND MORE APPLES

At first, the Pevensie children are grateful for the apple orchard when they find themselves stranded on the island. But eventually they grow tired of having nothing to eat but raw apples. In chapter 2, they try roasting the apples for variety. Here's how you can enjoy this tasty treat yourself!

Roasted Apples and Ice Cream

4 tbsp butter

2 tbsp lemon juice

2 tbsp apple juice or water

¾ cup packed light brown sugar

1/3 cup golden raisins

6 Granny Smith apples (1 ½ lbs)

1½ pints vanilla ice cream

1. Preheat oven to 425°.
2. Cut each of the apples in half; remove the cores.
3. Melt butter in a 2-quart saucepan on medium heat.
4. Add sugar, raisins, lemon juice, apple juice, stirring constantly until the sugar dissolves.
5. Pour sugar mixture into a baking pan (15 ½ x 10 ½).
6. Arrange apples in the pan, cut sides down. Roast in the oven for 20 minutes. (Do not turn the apples.)
7. Serve the warm apples and their syrup over ice cream.

More Fun Ways to Eat this Delicious Fruit:

- Enjoy apple slices with peanut butter, caramel, or cream cheese dip.
- Add small pieces (chunks or slices) to your cereal, yogurt, or fruit salad.
- Make your own applesauce using the following recipe.

Crock-Pot Applesauce

10 large apples—peeled, cored, and cut into slices/pieces/chunks

½ cup water

½ cup–1 cup sugar

1 tsp cinnamon

1. Mix all the ingredients in a large Crock-Pot.
2. Cover and cook on medium for 4–6 hours. (Higher heat will take less time; lower heat will take more.)
3. Stir from time to time.
4. Serve the applesauce warm over ice cream, or allow it to cool and enjoy it all by itself!

ASLAN'S HOW: MOSAICS AND MURALS

Aslan's How is a sacred memorial mound, built like a tomb over the ruins of the Stone Table. Inside are tunnels and caves lined with stones that form mosaics (patterns or pictures). Many feature a lion or some other ancient and mysterious symbol.

When the early church suffered persecution from the Roman emperors, they went underground—building miles of caves and tunnels and passages called "catacombs." They used the catacombs as a secret refuge, a place to meet for worship and prayer, and a place to bury their loved ones. Archaeologists have found these tunnels lined with mosaics depicting scenes from the life of Christ, as well as doves, fish, and other Christian symbols.

You can use an encyclopedia or the Internet to research more about the history of the catacombs and the mosaics that decorated their walls. Then try making a mosaic or mural of your own. You might enjoy illustrating scenes or symbols from *Prince Caspian* or one of your favorite Bible stories.

Mosaics: To make a mosaic, glue colorful beads or stones into a pattern—a picture—on heavy poster board. Another option: use sharp colored pencils or fine-tip markers to draw the pattern on graph paper, using geometric shapes (dots, circles, ovals, rectangles, squares) to imitate the look of beads or stones.

Murals: You can draw or paint a mural on butcher paper, packing paper, or bulletin board paper—any paper that comes in large sheets or rolls—and then pin it to the wall. Invite some friends to join you and make it a group project!

MAKE THE STORY YOUR OWN

- Draw a map of Narnia. Trace the journeys of the main characters or mark the locations where important things took place. Your map can be as small as a sheet of notebook paper or as large as a poster you hang on the wall.

- Create your own collection of poems inspired by characters or events in the book. Put them together in a booklet or journal that you decorate yourself.

- Plant an apple seed or an apple tree, just as Lilygloves, the Chief Mole, did for the kings and queens at Cair Paravel.

- Write a letter to a friend as if you are one of the main characters, such as Peter or Lucy, Prince Caspian or Doctor Cornelius. Tell your friend the story as if it happened to you.

- Choose a scene from the book and ask a few friends or classmates to act it out with you. Use props and costumes if you want to—or just use your imagination. Practice several times on your own, and then perform the scene for others.

- Make a model of a place such as the ruins of Cair Paravel, Trufflehunter's Cave, or the "lists"—the combat ring in which King Peter challenges King Miraz. Or create a diorama, a display with miniature figures and objects representing an important scene from the story.

- Design a series of bookmarks, each one featuring a specific person, place, or thing from the book. On the front, draw a picture of the subject. On the back, write a description, explaining its importance to the story. Give the bookmarks as gifts to your friends and family—or keep them for yourself!

READ THE OTHER BOOKS IN THE SERIES

Now that you've finished *Prince Caspian*, you'll want to read the rest of the great stories that make up C. S. Lewis's the Chronicles of Narnia. (By the way, Caspian's adventures continue in books 5 and 6.)

Book 1: *The Magician's Nephew*
Book 2: *The Lion, the Witch and the Wardrobe**
Book 3: *The Horse and His Boy*
Book 4: *Prince Caspian*
Book 5: *The Voyage of the Dawn Treader*
Book 6: *The Silver Chair*
Book 7: *The Last Battle*

**The Lion, the Witch and the Wardrobe* was actually the first book C. S. Lewis wrote about Narnia. Later he wrote six more, including a prequel explaining how Narnia came to be. At Lewis's suggestion, publishers renumbered the series to reflect the chronological order of the stories, rather than the publication date.

Book 1: *The Magician's Nephew:* Mad scientist or magician Andrew Ketterly gives his nephew, Digory Kirke, and neighbor-girl, Polly, two magic rings that will transport them into world after world beyond our own. Digory hopes he'll find a cure that will save his dying mother. Instead, he meets a great lion who sends him on an important quest. Will Digory obey Aslan's instructions, even when he doesn't understand—or will he listen to the secrets of a sorceress who promises to fulfill his wildest dreams?

Book 2: *The Lion, the Witch and the Wardrobe:* Peter, Susan, Edmund, and Lucy tumble through the door of a mysterious wardrobe at Professor Kirke's country home, only to find themselves in Narnia—a magical land held captive by the White Witch. It's she who makes it "always winter and never Christmas." But the children's appearance fulfills a prophecy signaling the end of the witch's reign. And the Great Lion Aslan is on the move. Could it be that Narnia's deliverance is at hand?

Book 3: *The Horse and His Boy:* Peter rules as High King over Narnia, and his brother and sisters sit as king and queens under him on the four thrones of Cair Paravel. Meanwhile in Calormen to the south, an orphaned peasant boy, a nobleman's daughter, and two talking horses plan a daring escape from a land of slavery. As their journey begins, the runaways un-cover a treacherous plot that could spell disaster for Narnia and all of its creatures. Will they manage to warn the kings and queens in time?

Book 4: *Prince Caspian.*

Book 5: *The Voyage of the Dawn Treader:* Edmund, Lucy, and their cousin Eustace join King Caspian on an epic ad-venture to find the friends and nobles his Uncle Miraz ban-ished from the kingdom long ago. Along the way, they'll meet slave traders, sea serpents, and stars who walk the earth. And Reepicheep the mouse will urge them all on to the end of the world—where he hopes to find Aslan's Country.

Book 6: *The Silver Chair:* King Caspian is brokenhearted. His only son has disappeared. Prince Rilian was last seen in the company of a beautiful enchantress. Wise old Narnians believe the prince has been kidnapped by one of those "northern witches" who are always plotting to overthrow their country.

The Great Lion Aslan sends Eustace and his schoolmate Jill on a quest to find and rescue the captive prince before it's too late.

Book 7: *The Last Battle:* Eustace and Jill learn that King Tirian needs help. Narnia is falling into the hands of its deadly enemies, the Calormenes. And the one behind its surrender appears to be Aslan himself! This cruel and vicious task-master is nothing like the Great Lion in the stories of old. Is it possible that he has changed so much? Or is this a deadly deception that will lead to Narnia's destruction? Is there any hope that Narnia can be saved?

Just as in *Prince Caspian*, there are "stories within the stories," profound spiritual truths and powerful life lessons, in each of these books. Keep your eyes open and see if you can discover them for yourself.

FIND OUT MORE

There are literally hundreds, if not thousands, of books, magazine articles, websites, radio programs, movies, and TV specials dedicated to celebrating the life and work of the beloved author of the Chronicles of Narnia, Christian apologist and theologian C. S. Lewis. Here are just a few to get you started:

Books about the Chronicles of Narnia

Ditchfield, Christin. *A Family Guide to Narnia: Biblical Truths in C. S. Lewis's the Chronicles of Narnia.* Wheaton, IL: Crossway Books, 2003.

Ditchfield, Christin. *A Christian Teacher's Guide to the Chronicles of Narnia.* Greensboro, NC: Carson-Dellosa Publishing Company, 2008.

Duriez, Colin. *A Field Guide to Narnia.* Downer's Grove, IL: InterVarsity Press, 2004.

Ford, Paul F. *Companion to Narnia*, Revised Edition: *A Complete Guide to the Magical World of C. S. Lewis's the Chronicles of Narnia.* San Francisco: HarperCollins, 2005.

Sibley, Brian. *The Land of Narnia*. San Francisco: Harper-Collins, 1998.

Books about C. S. Lewis

Cording, Ruth James. *C. S. Lewis: A Celebration of His Early Life*. Nashville: Broadman & Holman, 2000.

Dorsett, Lyle W. and Marjorie Lamp Mead. *C. S. Lewis: Letters to Children*. New York: Simon & Schuster, 1996.

Duriez, Colin. *Tolkien and C. S. Lewis: The Gift of Friendship*. Mahwah, NJ: Paulist Press, 2003.

Duriez, Colin. *The C. S. Lewis Chronicles: The Indispensable Biography of the Creator of Narnia Full of Little-Known Facts, Events and Miscellany*. New York: Bluebridge, 2005.

Gresham, Douglas. *Lenten Lands: My Childhood with Joy Davidman and C. S. Lewis*. San Francisco: Harper-Collins, 2003.

Peters, Thomas C. *Simply C. S. Lewis: A Beginner's Guide to the Life and Works of C. S. Lewis*. Wheaton, IL: Crossway Books, 1997.

Websites for Narnia Fans

The Official Site of the Chronicles of Narnia: www.narnia.com

Explore the breathtaking fantasy world of C. S. Lewis on the Web: www.thelionscall.com

The C. S. Lewis Foundation: www.cslewis.org

The HarperCollins C. S. Lewis site: www.cslewisclassics. com

Other Media

C. S. Lewis: Beyond Narnia. A brief documentary appropriate for families, starring Anton Rodgers and directed by Norman Stone for Faith and Values Media and the Hallmark Channel. Available on DVD.

The Chronicles of Narnia: Prince Caspian. A new movie by Walden/Disney, summer 2008. Information: www.walden.com.

The Chronicles of Narnia. Audio recordings of all seven books by the award-winning producers of Focus on the Family Radio Theatre, available on cassette or compact disc. For more information, call 1-800-A-FAMILY.

Places to Visit

The Marion E. Wade Center at Wheaton College, Wheaton, Illinois. This international study and research center houses the world's largest collection of C. S. Lewis's letters, manuscripts, audio and video tapes, dissertations, artwork, periodicals, photographs, and memorabilia. For information on tours, call 630-752-5908 or visit www.wheaton.edu/wadecenter/.

The Kilns at Oxford, England. Each year, thousands of tourists visit C. S. Lewis's home in Oxfordshire, England. For photographs of the site and information on tours, visit www.cslewsistours.co.uk.

Christin Ditchfield is an accomplished educator, author, conference speaker, and host of the internationally syndicated radio program, Take It To Heart!™ Using real life stories, rich word pictures, biblical illustrations, and touches of humor, Christin calls believers to enthusiastically seek after God, giving them practical tools to help deepen their personal relationship with Christ.

Christin's articles have appeared in numerous national and international magazines such as *Focus on the Family, Today's Christian Woman, Sports Spectrum,* and *Power for Living.* She writes the "Everyday Theology" column for *Today's Christian.* Christin has also written dozens of gospel tracts for Good News Publishers, including *Under Attack* (9/11) and *The Passion of Jesus Christ,* each of which has sold more than a million copies worldwide. Christin is a frequent guest on radio and television programs such as *Open Line, Midday Connection, HomeWord with Jim Burns,* and Dr. D. James Kennedy's *Truths That Transform.* She is the author of more than fifty books, including *A Family Guide to Narnia* and *A Family Guide to the Bible.*

For more information, visit Christin's ministry website at www.TakeItToHeartRadio.com.